Xtreme Adventure

TREASURE HUNTING

BY S.L. HAMILTON

EDGE
FRANKLIN WATTS

LONDON·SYDNEY

Franklin Watts
First published in Great Britain in 2015 by The Watts Publishing Group

First published in the USA by ABDO Publishing Company.

Editor: John Hamilton
Graphic Design: Sue Hamilton
Cover Design: Sue Hamilton

Acknowledgements:
Cover Photo: Alamy
Interior Photos: AP-pgs 6-7, 12-13, 14, 15, 16 (inset), 20, 21, 23, 24, 25, 26 &
32; Corbis-pg 19 (top); Getty Images-pgs 8-9, 10-11, 18, 28 & 30-31; National
Geographic-pgs 22 & 27; Science Source-pgs 4-5 & 19 (bottom); Thinkstock-pgs
1, 2-3, 16-17 & 29.

Every attempt has been made to clear copyright. Should there be any inadvertent
omission please apply to the publisher for rectification.

Dewey number 622.1'9
HB ISBN 978 1 4451 3959 3
Library ebook ISBN 978 1 4451 3963 0

Printed in China

Franklin Watts
An imprint of
Hachette Children's Group
Part of The Watts Publishing Group
Carmelite House
50 Victoria Embankment
London EC4Y 0DZ

An Hachette UK Company
www.hachette.co.uk

www.franklinwatts.co.uk

CONTENTS

TREASURE HUNTING

Treasure hunters search underwater and on land. They look for treasure such as gold, silver, jewellery and even historical artefacts.

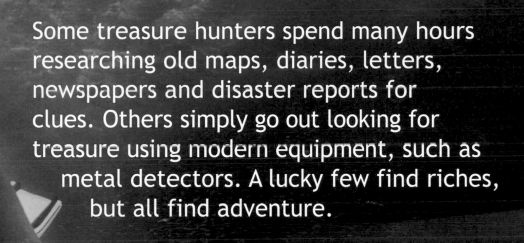

Some treasure hunters spend many hours researching old maps, diaries, letters, newspapers and disaster reports for clues. Others simply go out looking for treasure using modern equipment, such as metal detectors. A lucky few find riches, but all find adventure.

XTREME FACT – The most valuable treasure hunter's find was the wreck of the Spanish galleon *Nuestra Señora de Atocha in 1985. The treasure is valued at more than £300 million.*

Tools & Equipment

A treasure hunter's most useful tool is a metal detector with headphones. There are metal detectors made for use on land and some for underwater. The detector sends an audio or vibration signal to the searcher. Many of today's detectors also have a visual display that points to what may be buried.

XTREME FACT– Treasure hunters spend a lot of time walking. Good shoes, a mobile phone, a handheld GPS device, extra batteries and water are important items to carry.

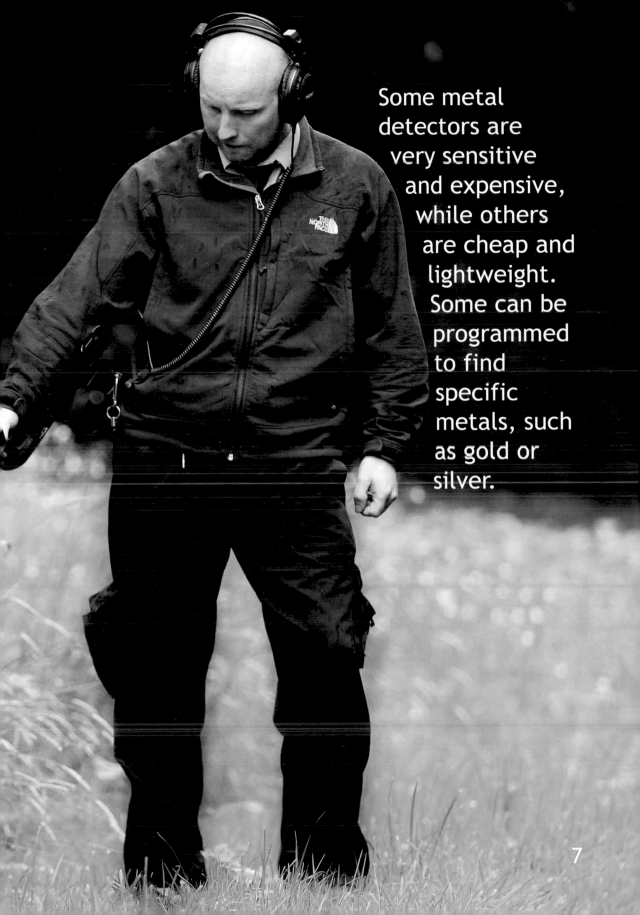

Some metal detectors are very sensitive and expensive, while others are cheap and lightweight. Some can be programmed to find specific metals, such as gold or silver.

Underwater treasure hunters need diving skills and scuba gear. Some treasure hunters use a device called a 'mailbox blower'. Treasure hunter Mel Fisher came up with the idea when he wanted the ocean's clear water near the surface to be blown down to the often murky bottom. Clear water would help divers see better. The blower also blew away layers of sand, sometimes uncovering important artefacts and clues.

XTREME FACT – Blowers have caused 6–9-metre-wide and 0.6–0.9-metre-deep holes in the ocean floor. Some people say using blowers damages sea habitats.

DANGERS

Some treasure hunters travel deep into forests or walk to remote beaches and shorelines. It's the thrill of finding treasure that is so exciting, but they may get lost or hurt. They wear sensible clothing and footwear, and take a first-aid kit.

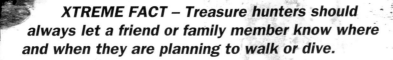

XTREME FACT – Treasure hunters should always let a friend or family member know where and when they are planning to walk or dive.

Underwater treasure hunters must be skilled divers. They always dive with a partner. There is the risk of drowning or becoming trapped in a wreck.

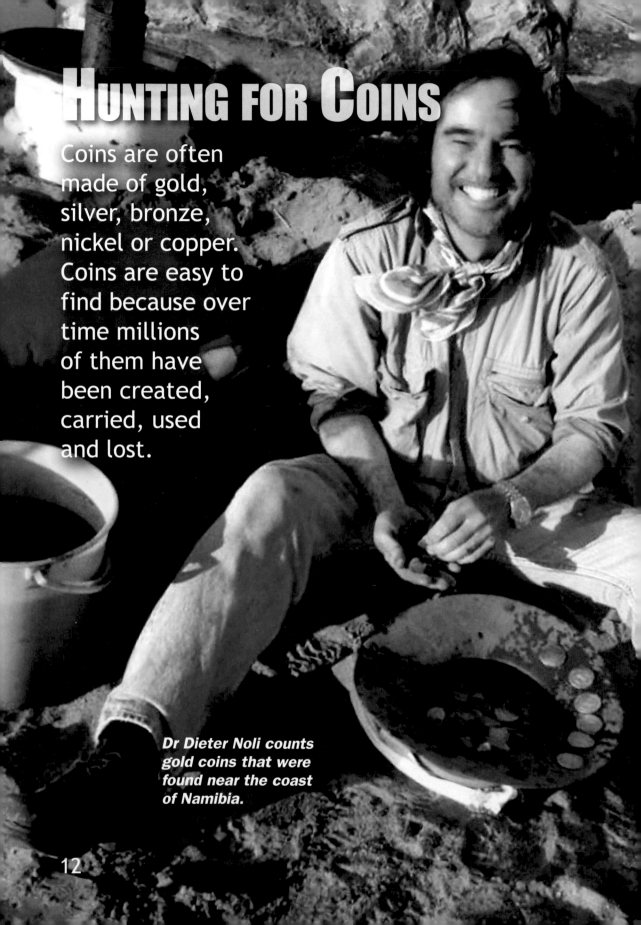

HUNTING FOR COINS

Coins are often made of gold, silver, bronze, nickel or copper. Coins are easy to find because over time millions of them have been created, carried, used and lost.

Dr Dieter Noli counts gold coins that were found near the coast of Namibia.

Coin hunters are often seen searching parks, beaches and old shipwrecks. Some coins are not worth more than their face value, but finding them is still a fun adventure. However, every coin hunter searches for the 'big find'.

A big find includes coins that are rare, old or unusual. Coins that were hammered or milled are valuable finds. Cast coins with a mistake on them, or ones that were made in small numbers, are also treasure.

XTREME FACT – People who look for old coins are called 'coin shooters'.

Archaeologist Alan Graham excavates the Frome Hoard from a field in England.

In April 2010, treasure hunter Dave Crisp found a hoard (collection) of coins in a clay pot buried in a field near the town of Frome, Somerset. Rather than dig it up himself, Crisp alerted archaeologists. The Frome Hoard turned out to be 52,503 silver and bronze Roman coins from the 3rd century CE. It became one of the largest collections of coins ever found in Great Britain.

The Frome Hoard is on display at the Museum of Somerset. It is valued at more than £320,000. Sometimes, coin hunting can make the treasure hunter rich!

A cleaned Roman silver denarius is held next to unwashed Roman coins from the Frome Hoard.

XTREME FACT – There are more 'lost' coins than coins being used today.

HUNTING FOR JEWELLERY

Beaches are popular jewellery hunting spots. People drop precious jewellery, for example sunblock makes hands slippery and rings can slip off easily. Beach treasure hunters with metal detectors have found diamond rings and bracelets, gold rings and watches, pearl earrings and pins, and even jewelled necklaces.

Roy Evans displays some of the treasure he has found in the sand of his local beach.

XTREME FACT – Some treasure hunters not only find expensive jewellery, but many also go on a hunt to find the original owner. Sometimes the reward is returning a lost item to its owner.

Shipwrecks have yielded many amazing jewellery finds, including necklaces, rings and pins.

An emerald and gold cross salvaged in 1986 from the shipwreck Nuestra Señora de Atocha, which sank in 1622.

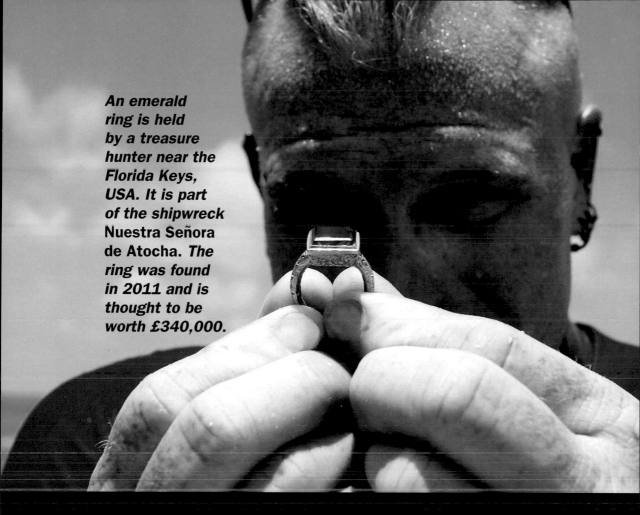

An emerald ring is held by a treasure hunter near the Florida Keys, USA. It is part of the shipwreck **Nuestra Señora de Atocha.** *The ring was found in 2011 and is thought to be worth £340,000.*

An emerald brooch from the **Nuestra Señora de las Maravillas.** *The Spanish ship sank in 1656 off Grand Bahama Island, about 90 km off Florida, USA. While items have been found, the wreck area is still being searched today.*

HUNTING FOR SILVER

Silver was commonly transported in ships. It is very valuable. Silver coins, ingots and bars have been discovered in several shipwrecks. The SS *Gairsoppa*, a merchant ship sunk during World War II off the coast of Ireland, yielded 1,203 bars of silver valued at about £25 million.

Treasure hunters bring up silver bars from the SS Gairsoppa.

The Spanish ship *La Capitana* struck a reef
and sank in 1654. Most of its cargo of silver
ingots and coins was salvaged soon after
the ship sank. Using the diary of a survivor,
treasure hunters rediscovered *La Capitana*
off the coast of Ecuador in 1996. They
salvaged nearly 4,000 silver coins, two silver
ingots, and other artefacts valued at over
£170 million.

HUNTING FOR GOLD

Finding gold is a treasure hunter's dream come true. Gold coins, bars and jewellery are sometimes found in shipwrecks.

Treasure hunter David Booth is shown with the 2,000-year-old gold neck 'torcs' he discovered with his metal detector.

Some metal detectors can be programmed to find gold. Many treasure hunters look for gold objects in the ground. Others use their metal detectors to search for the raw metal in streams or rivers. After a positive signal, treasure hunters pan for gold flakes and nuggets. It's very hard work!

A rich pay-off of gold flakes and nuggets from a treasure hunt.

Treasure hunters pan for gold.

Hunting for Glass & Bottles

Glass containers that once held medicines, snuff, ink, alcohol, milk, fruits or vegetables are valuable treasure. Antique bottles and ceramic jugs are often found in old rubbish tips, toilet pits or gardens. These items are pieces of history and are treasured by collectors.

A treasure hunter digs in an old outside toilet pit.

A glass bottle for Warner's Safe Kidney & Liver Cure and a ceramic jug are among the finds from an outside toilet pit. These items may be worth £18–200 each.

HUNTING FOR ARTEFACTS

Artefacts are anything of a historical nature, such as arrowheads, pottery or medals. Treasure hunters search areas where ancient people lived or where battles were fought. Archaeologists, scientists and historians with special training may be employed to properly excavate an important find. Museums are often the purchasers of these treasured relics.

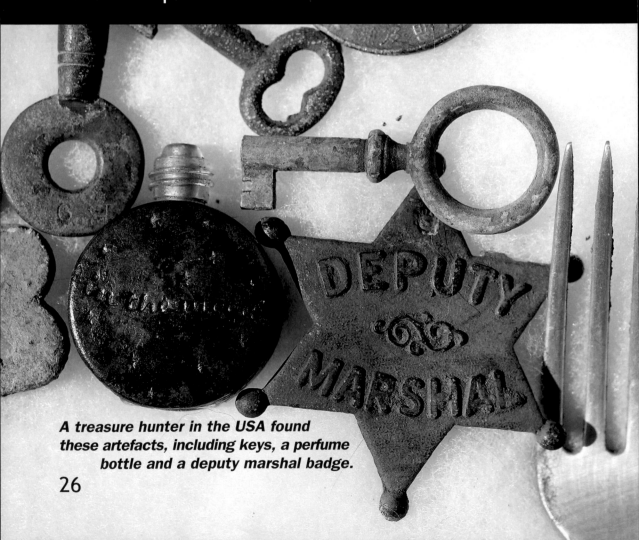

A treasure hunter in the USA found these artefacts, including keys, a perfume bottle and a deputy marshal badge.

XTREME FACT – As much as 90 per cent of archaeological artefacts are found by treasure hunters.

A collection of metal and clay artefacts found in a Spanish shipwreck.

WHERE TO HUNT

Luck, persistence, patience and research can lead to discovering treasure. People of all ages have found great historical artefacts. Most beaches and parks are public property, and are good places to hunt. National parks, gardens and forests have rules to stop people digging. It is important to find out about any rules before treasure hunting.

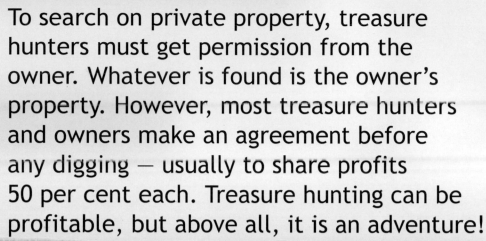

To search on private property, treasure hunters must get permission from the owner. Whatever is found is the owner's property. However, most treasure hunters and owners make an agreement before any digging — usually to share profits 50 per cent each. Treasure hunting can be profitable, but above all, it is an adventure!

GLOSSARY

ARCHAEOLOGIST
A person who searches for, uncovers and studies artefacts from the past in order to learn how people of ancient societies once lived.

ARTEFACTS
Objects made or owned by a person or group of people. Often of historical interest, artefacts can be: something worn, such as clothing or jewellery; something used, such as dishes or tools; or something created by a culture, such as art.

CAST COINS
Coins made by pouring melted metal into a mould.

FACE VALUE
The actual value printed on the face of a coin.

GPS (GLOBAL POSITIONING SYSTEM)
A system of orbiting satellites that transmits information to GPS receivers on Earth. Using information from the satellites, receivers can calculate location, speed and direction with great accuracy.

HAMMERED COIN
A coin made by placing a metal disk (usually gold or silver) between two shaped dies (often wooden) and striking the top die with a hammer. Hammered coins were used in Europe, the Middle East and the New World between about 600 CE to 1700 CE.

Ingot
A block of metal made by melting a metal, such as silver or gold, and pouring it into a mould. Ingots are a specific quality (purity), weight and size.

Milled Coin
A coin made by a machine known as a mill. The edges of the coin are often raised or have vertical grooves.

Salvage
Recovering lost cargo and other items, such as from a shipwreck.

Snuff
Powered tobacco sniffed up a person's nostril, most popular in the 17th century.

Torc
A band of twisted metal that is worn around the neck.

World War II
A war that was fought from 1939 to 1945, involving countries around the world.

INDEX